MW01165190

HOME

Sweet

PLANET

SUPER SCIENCE

JODIE MANGOR

Rourke
Educational Media
rourkeeducationalmedia.com

A Division of
Carson
Dellosa
Education

Before Reading: *Building Background Knowledge and Vocabulary*

Building background knowledge can help children process new information and build upon what they already know. Before reading a book, it is important to tap into what children already know about the topic. This will help them develop their vocabulary and increase their reading comprehension.

Questions and Activities to Build Background Knowledge:

1. Look at the front cover of the book and read the title. What do you think this book will be about?
2. What do you already know about this topic?
3. Take a book walk and skim the pages. Look at the table of contents, photographs, captions, and bold words. Did these text features give you any information or predictions about what you will read in this book?

Vocabulary: *Vocabulary Is Key to Reading Comprehension*

Use the following directions to prompt a conversation about each word.

- Read the vocabulary words.
- What comes to mind when you see each word?
- What do you think each word means?

Vocabulary Words:
- biofuels
- climate change
- elements
- fossil fuel
- gadgets
- greenhouse gases
- organic
- toxic

During Reading: *Reading for Meaning and Understanding*

To achieve deep comprehension of a book, children are encouraged to use close reading strategies. During reading, it is important to have children stop and make connections. These connections result in deeper analysis and understanding of a book.

 Close Reading a Text

During reading, have children stop and talk about the following:

- Any confusing parts
- Any unknown words
- Text to text, text to self, text to world connections
- The main idea in each chapter or heading

Encourage children to use context clues to determine the meaning of any unknown words. These strategies will help children learn to analyze the text more thoroughly as they read.

When you are finished reading this book, turn to the next-to-last page for **Text-Dependent Questions** and an **Extension Activity**.

TABLE OF CONTENTS

EASY LIVING

We are very lucky. We live in a time with many conveniences.

Plastic forks, electronic **gadgets**, you name it. These things save us time and effort. They affect the ways we work, shop, and play.

We are so used to these things that we may not always notice them.

They make our lives easier. But are they always good? Let's look at some conveniences up close.

Time to Play
We use electronics to do fun things. We watch movies, play video games, or play with smart toys. But old electronics can leak **toxic** wastes.

THROW IT AWAY!

What do you do when you have a runny nose? You can grab a tissue and wipe your nose with it. Then into the trash it goes.

Paper products are great for gross messes. Paper towels work well for cleaning up your pet's accidents. Napkins keep your face and hands clean. Paper plates and cups make picnics easy. And what would we do without toilet paper?

Get Creative with Cloth
You can help save energy and resources. Use cloth instead of paper products! Rags and cloth napkins can be washed and used over and over again.

We use these things and throw them away. But paper products take huge amounts of energy to make. And they create a lot of waste.

Plastic is an amazing invention. It is strong and light. It can be molded into many shapes. Look around you. It's everywhere! Plastic wrap helps keep our food fresh. We use plastic bags to carry many things. If we get thirsty, we can buy plastic bottles filled with water.

Reduce, Reuse, Recycle
You can help keep plastic out of landfills and the environment. Recycle and use fewer disposable items.

The world makes 335 million tons (304 billion kilograms) of plastic every year. This uses a lot of **fossil fuel**. It contributes to **climate change**. A lot of plastic gets thrown away. But plastic doesn't decompose like paper. It can last hundreds of years. It gets into the environment and stays there for a long, long time.

Warming Earth
Climate change is the process of Earth heating up. This is mostly caused by the burning of fossil fuels. The gases released create a sort of blanket in the atmosphere, keeping the sun's heat from escaping back out into space.

PLUG IT IN

Electricity is a big part of our lives. Look around your house. What's plugged into the outlets? A refrigerator. Lights. You might also have a dishwasher, a TV, and more. Can you imagine living without these things?

Making and sharing electricity affects the environment. Some power plants burn coal, natural gas, or oil. This produces **greenhouse gases**. These contribute to climate change. Some power plants use nuclear energy. This makes dangerous waste. Electricity can also be made from the wind, sun, or water. But these sources can only make electricity when they are available.

Flip It Off
To save energy, turn things off when you're not using them. Click lights off as you leave the room. You'll save money too!

Chances are you know a lot of people who have cell phones.

They make it easy to keep in touch. You can text or call anywhere, any place. Cell phones are useful in emergencies. You can also use them to take photos, check the internet, and more. They are a very convenient thing to have.

But cell phones are made with rare earth **elements**. Gathering these materials damages the environment. Harmful chemicals are needed to process them.

Phone Zone
It is very important to recycle phones. Precious materials can be removed and used again. This is better than mining for them.

Lithium, a metal in cell phone batteries, comes from mines like this one.

The internet is a great place for learning. You can find huge amounts of information. There are educational books, videos, and games.

But the more kids use computers, the less active they are. They are spending less time outside. They are less connected to nature.

Unplug
Nature is also a great place to learn! The more time you spend in nature, the more you will understand and care about it.

RIGHT TO YOU

Want to buy that hard-to-find game? Before, you had to drive from store to store to look for an item. Now you can look online. Click a button and it will be delivered to your front door. It's so easy!

But online orders lead to more traffic. Delivery trucks pollute the air. They release greenhouse gases and contribute to climate change.

Shop 'til You Drop
Make your shopping better for the environment. Buy from local stores. Walk or bike there.

Need to go somewhere? With modern cars, trains, buses, and airplanes, we can go faster and farther than ever before. But most of these vehicles are powered by fossil fuels. They pollute the air. The pollution can hurt our health. It can affect our hearts and lungs.

Petroleum, a fossil fuel, is used to make jet fuel.

Many designers are working hard to make vehicles that are better for the environment. Some newer cars are powered by **biofuels**. These fuels are made from food crops and other **organic** waste. Other cars are powered by electricity. And more new ideas are in the works.

Get There
For short distances, walk or bike. Take a bus or other public transportation if you can.

Turn on a tap, and water comes out. Running water is a convenience most of us take for granted. We use it for drinking, cooking, and cleaning.

Imagine life without indoor plumbing. In many places, people have to haul water. The amount of fresh water on Earth is limited. Only so much is available for us to use.

In India, some women and girls spend hours each day carrying water to their homes.

Don't Waste a Drop!
You can save water at home. Don't let the faucet run while you brush your teeth or wash the dishes. Use just the water you need.

ACTIVITY

Old to New

Turn an empty plastic bottle into a cute and creative planter! You'll keep the bottle out of the waste stream and add a little green to your life.

Supplies

- empty plastic bottles
- scissors
- paint
- paintbrushes
- glue
- tape
- string
- yarn or pipe cleaners
- markers
- pebbles
- potting soil
- a small plant

Directions

1. Look at your plastic bottle. Decide how you are going to turn it into a planter. What will it look like? An animal? A person's face?

2. Have an adult help you cut any holes you need into the container.

3. Use the art supplies to decorate the container.

4. Put a few pebbles in the bottom of the container. Fill it with potting soil.

5. Plant a small plant in your planter.

6. Give it some water and watch it grow.

GLOSSARY

biofuels (BYE-oh-fyoo-uhls): fuels made from renewable materials such as plants or animal waste

climate change (KLYE-mit chaynj): changes in Earth's weather patterns, including global warming

elements (EL-uh-muhnts): natural substances that cannot be divided into simpler substances

fossil fuel (FAH-suhl FYOO-uhl): fuel (such as coal, oil, or natural gas) formed deep inside Earth from plant or animal remains

gadgets (GAJ-its): small tools that do a particular job

greenhouse gases (GREEN-hous GAS-uhs): gases that contribute to global warming, such as carbon dioxide and methane

organic (or-GAN-ik): from or produced by living things

toxic (TAHK-sik): poisonous

INDEX

TEXT-DEPENDENT QUESTIONS

1. Name three conveniences that many people take for granted.

2. How can cell phones harm the environment?

3. What are some positive and negative sides of using plastic products?

4. What are two different sources of power used to make electricity?

5. Name three ways to conserve water in your home.

EXTENSION ACTIVITY

Make a list of all the things around your home that use energy. Now brainstorm ways to use less energy. Can you open curtains to let in sunlight instead of turning on the lights? Or dry your clothes on a line instead of in a dryer? What other ways can you save energy? Share your ideas with your family.

ABOUT THE AUTHOR

Jodie Mangor writes magazine articles and books for children. She is also the author of audio tour scripts for high-profile museums and tourist destinations around the world. Many of these tours are for kids. She lives in Ithaca, New York, with her family.

www.rourkeeducationalmedia.com

PHOTO CREDITS: page 3, 22: ©ManAsThep; page 4(a): ©Scukrov; page 4(b): ©BrianAJackson; page 4(c): ©Luhuanfeng; page 5: ©baona; page 6: ©Kristian Sekulic; page 7: ©Detailfoto; page 8-9: ©panaramka; page 8: ©JaniBryson; page 9(b): ©luigigiodano; page 10: ©hikesterson; page 11: ©zhonggou; page 12: ©Mark Bowden; page 13: ©Skyhobo; page 13(b): ©Phaelnogueira; pages 14-15: ©Fertnig; page 15: ©Avalon_Studio; pages 16-17: ©DarthArt; page 17: ©huePhotography; page 18: ©lowellSannes; page 18(b): ©Hirkophoto; page 19: ©LeManna; page 20: ©hadynyah; page 20(b): ©dentalfilled; page 21: ©undefined undefined

Edited by: Kim Thompson
Cover and interior design by: Rhea Magaro-Wallace

Library of Congress PCN Data

Home Sweet Planet / Jodie Mangor
(Super Science)
  ISBN 978-1-73161-433-9 (hard cover)
  ISBN 978-1-73161-228-1 (soft cover)
  ISBN 978-1-73161-538-1 (e-Book)
  ISBN 978-1-73161-643-2 (ePub)
Library of Congress Control Number: 2019932075

Rourke Educational Media
Printed in the United States of America,
North Mankato, Minnesota

Oct19
J
363.7

24